Special Symbols:

This book is organized to guide the individual through the training. In addition to the Notes section there are a number of symbols used to help the participant throughout the presentation and workshop. For your convenience these symbols are repeated at the introduction of each section of this workbook.

Suggestion:

This symbol represents a suggestion or is a general statement relating to facilitation of the training.

Tip:

This symbol represents a tip to the Facilitator and is specific to the concept that the Facilitator is presenting.

Question:

This symbol represents a question that may be asked to the Facilitator or to the participants in the workshop. It is intended to foster interaction during the training.

Table of Contents

Introduction

Section 1

Section 2

Section 3

Appendix

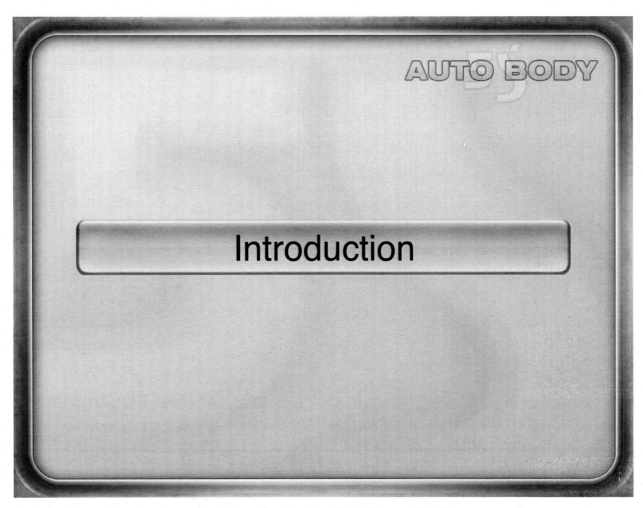

AUTO BODY 5S

Introduction

Participant Workbook

In this Section

- Learn the 5S's
- Introduction to the workshop layout

Participant Workbook Provided To:

_____

 Suggestion   **Tip**   **Question**

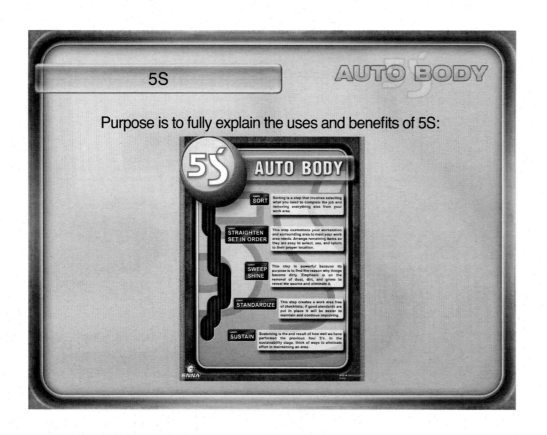

Notes, Slide 1:

_____

_____

_____

_____

_____

_____

Notes, Slide 1 continued:

_____

_____

_____

_____

_____

_____

Tip:

Pay particular attention to the Facilitator when learning about a clean operation.

Question:

What do people generally think of an operation that is clean?

_____

_____

_____

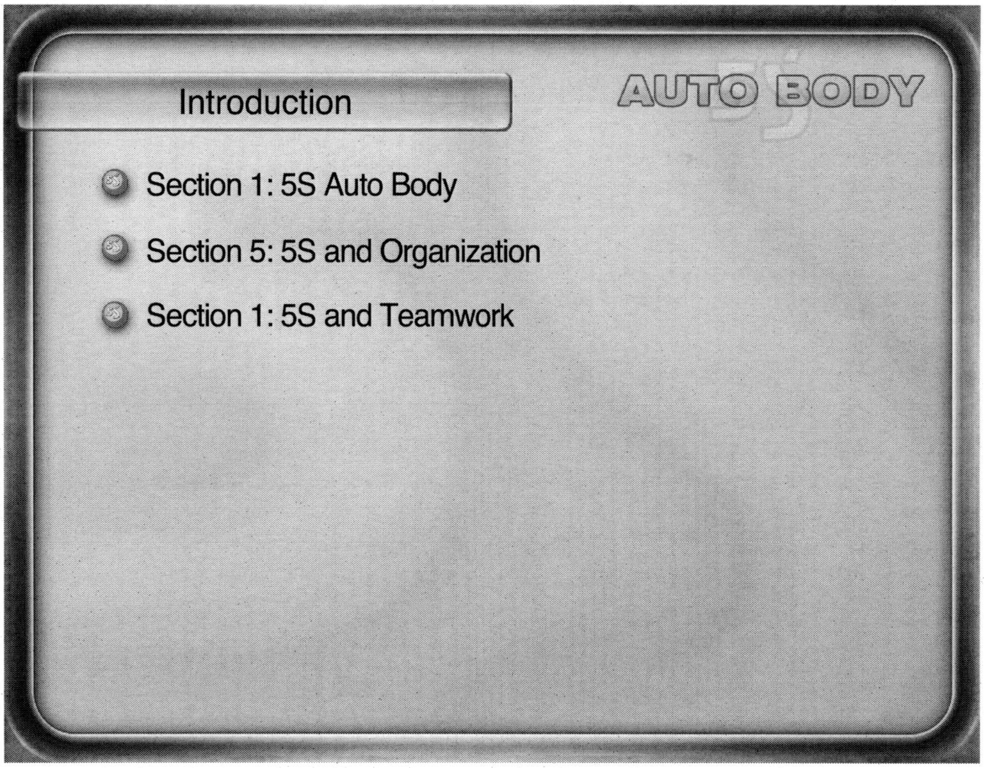

Introduction

AUTO BODY

- Section 1: 5S Auto Body
- Section 5: 5S and Organization
- Section 1: 5S and Teamwork

Notes, Slide 2:

_____

_____

_____

_____

_____

_____

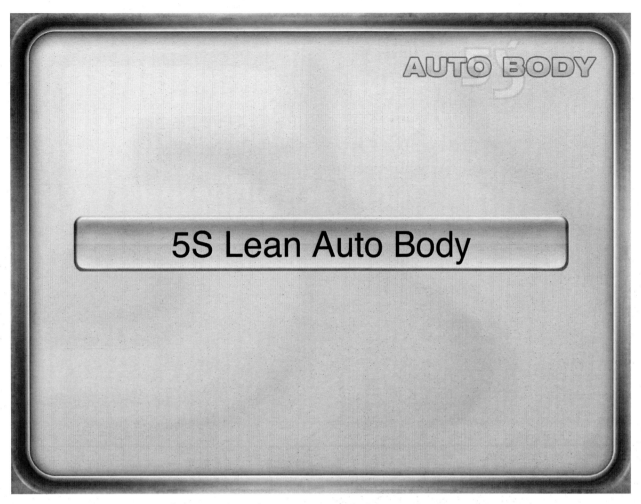

Participant Workbook

In this Section

- Learn the context of 5S
- Discover how 5S fits into improvement projects
- Study the 8 Wastes of Lean Auto Body

Participant Workbook Provided To:

_____

 Suggestion   **Tip**   **Question**

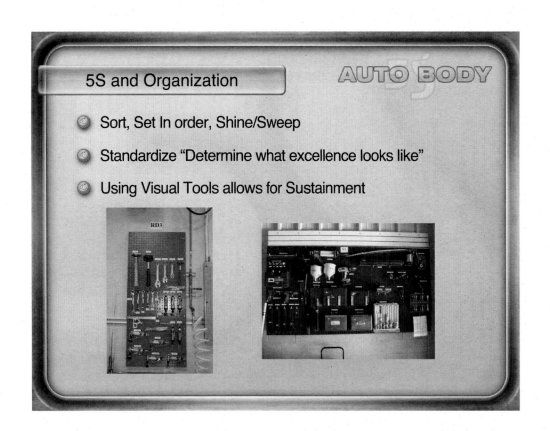

Notes, Slide 4:

_____

_____

_____

_____

_____

_____

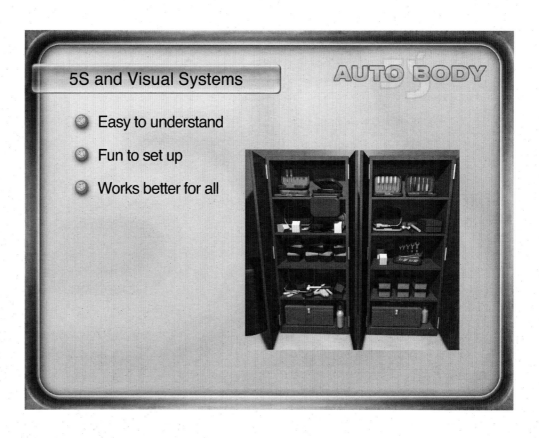

Notes, Slide 5:

_____

_____

_____

_____

_____

_____

Question:

Can you think of any kind of job that may require the need to be visual?

_____

_____

_____

Why 5S

- Allows us to maintain a more organized area
- Able to clean less and clean easier
- Makes our work are more productive
  - Makes the 8 Wastes obvious
  - Creates a standard for improvement
  - A way to get many people involved
  - Low real cost, high-impact for company

AUTO BODY

Notes, Slide 6:

_____

_____

_____

_____

_____

Question:

Why are we doing 5S?

_____

_____

_____

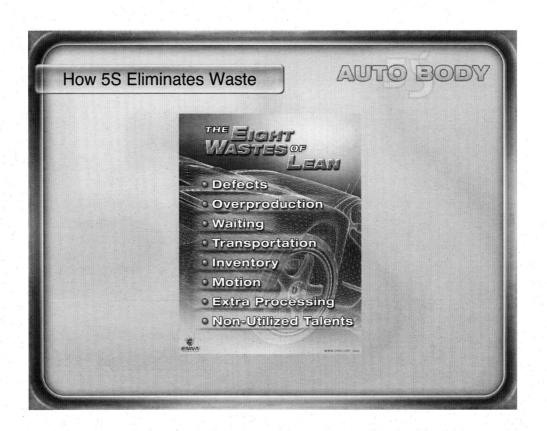

Notes, Slide 7:

_____

_____

_____

_____

_____

_____

Tip:
Focus on the 8 Wastes and what the definitions are.

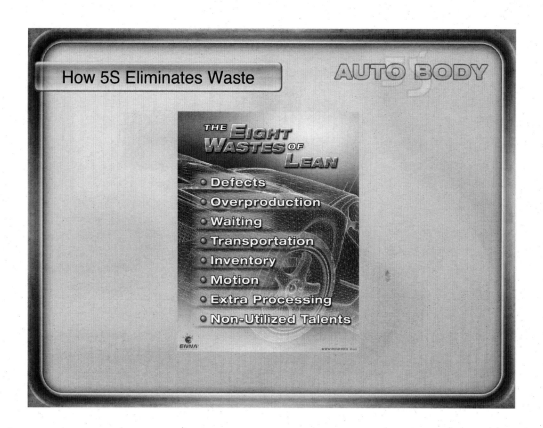

How 5S Eliminates Waste

Notes, Slide 7 continued:

_____

_____

_____

_____

_____

_____

Tip:
The 8 Wastes are a fundamental building block of 5S. Ask the facilitator to fully explain the wastes so that you understand them completely.

Overproduction

The act of producing more than necessary, including performing work out of order or too fast.

Examples:
- Working on too many estimates at one time or in the wrong order
- Working on parts for a vehicle that is not scheduled to come in for days or weeks

Notes, Slide 8:

_____

_____

_____

_____

Waste Definition: _____

_____

Additional Example: _____

_____

Tip:
Operations should look at ways to only produce what is truly needed. Anything more will result in loss of efficiency and effectiveness.

Question:
Why is overproduction so detrimental to an organization?

_____

_____

_____

AUTO BODY

Activity that adds no value to the product or service from the viewpoint of the customer.

Examples:
- Buffing a bumper longer than necessary
- Additional verifying and checking in the estimating process
- Preparing a job to be worked on by the next department without knowing what is needed

Notes, Slide 9:

_____

_____

_____

_____

Waste Definition: _____

_____

Additional Example: _____

_____

Tip:
This is the hardest waste to find. However, the solution is simple. If you think about it, if it is truly a waste of over processing, then the ultimate solution is to find a way to not do it.

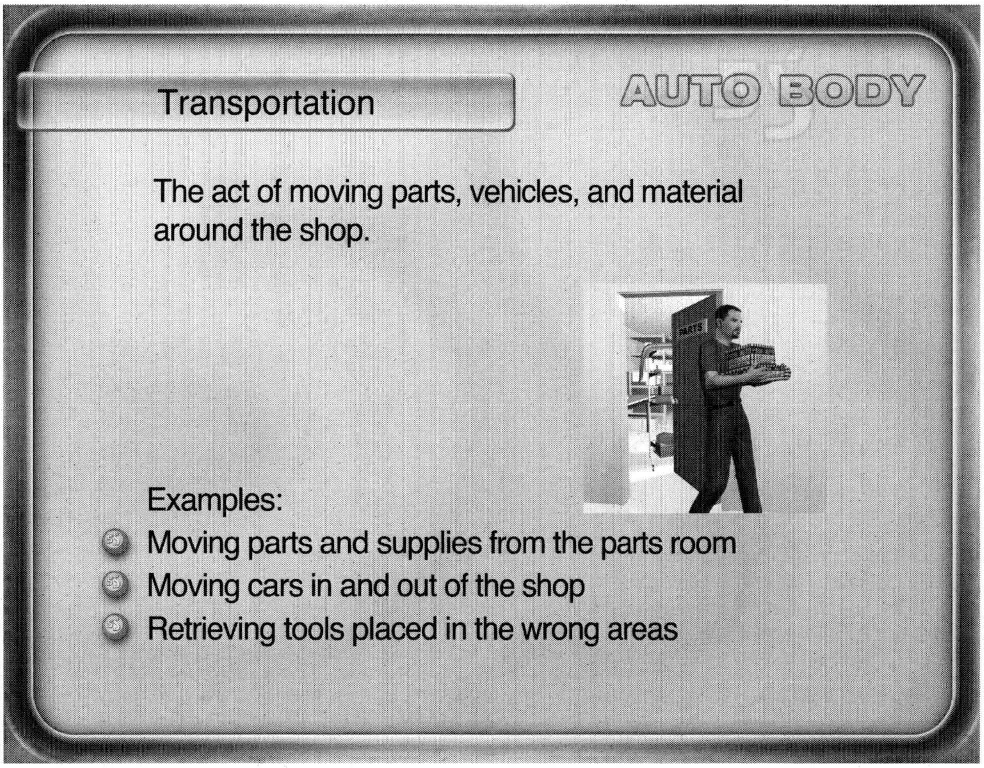

Notes, Slide 10:

____

____

____

____

Waste Definition: ____

____

Additional Example: ____

____

Motion

AUTO BODY

Any movement of technicians without a productive result.

Examples:
- Stopping work to go look for misplaced tools
- Going to the parts department to pick up parts
- Searching for management or other technicians

Notes, Slide 11:

_____

_____

_____

_____

Waste Definition: _____

_____

Additional Example: _____

_____

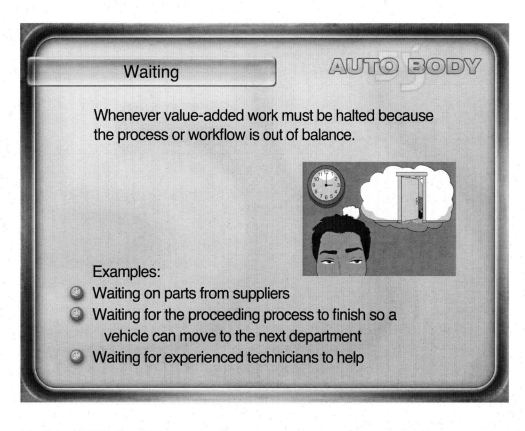

Notes, Slide 12:

_____

_____

_____

_____

Tip:
Try purposely waiting rather than doing something. It is hard to wait.

Waste Definition: _____

_____

Additional Example: _____

_____

Question:

What are some times that you have waited? What are you waiting for?

_____

_____

_____

Defects/Rejects

AUTO BODY

Any re-work, including after it has left the shop and is returned, quality errors, or mistakes.

Examples:
- Painting the wrong part
- Installing the wrong part on the wrong car
- Re-paint or re-buff a job

Notes, Slide 13:

_____

_____

_____

_____

Waste Definition: _____

_____

Additional Example: _____

_____

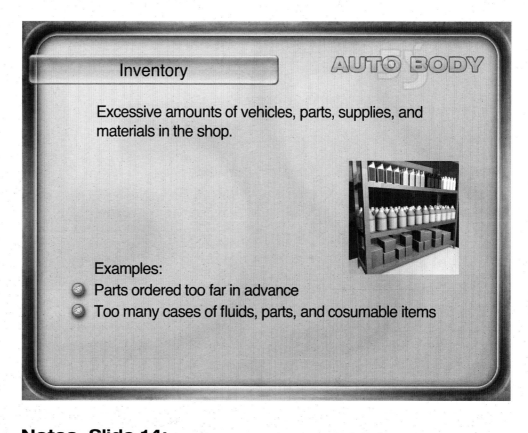

Notes, Slide 14:

_____

_____

_____

_____

Waste Definition: _____

_____

Additional Example: _____

_____

Question:

What are the three stages that inventory lives as in your company?

_____

_____

_____

Non-Utilized Talents

AUTO BODY

The act of not properly utilizing technicians to the best of their abilities.

Examples:
- Not cross training technicians
- Not giving assistance to technicians who are actively seeking to improve the flow in their area

Notes, Slide 15:

_____

_____

_____

_____

Waste Definition: _____

_____

Additional Example: _____

_____

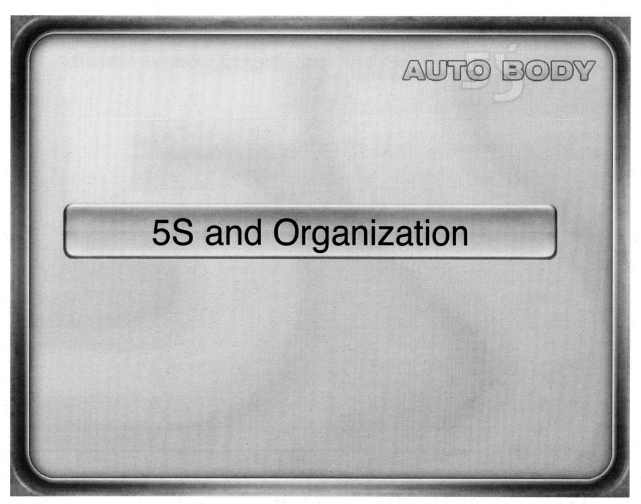

5S and Organization

Participant Workbook

In this Section

- The meaning behind 5S
- Applying 5S in your area and environment
- The five elements of 5S
- Guide for participants through the proper sequence of learning 5S

 Suggestion   **Tip**   **Question**

5 Words that Begin with S

Notes, Slide 17:

_____

_____

_____

_____

_____

_____

Question:

Why are we doing 5S?

_____

_____

_____

Notes, Slide 18:

_____

_____

_____

_____

Tip:
When sorting, make two categories:
1) what is needed for the job, and
2) everything else.

Sort Action Defined: _____

_____

Additional Example: _____

_____

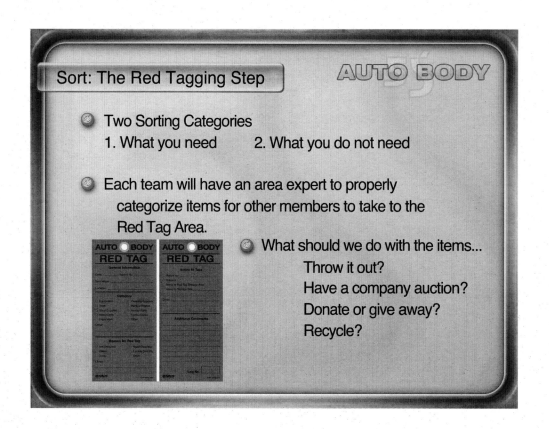

Notes, Slide 19:

_____

_____

_____

_____

_____

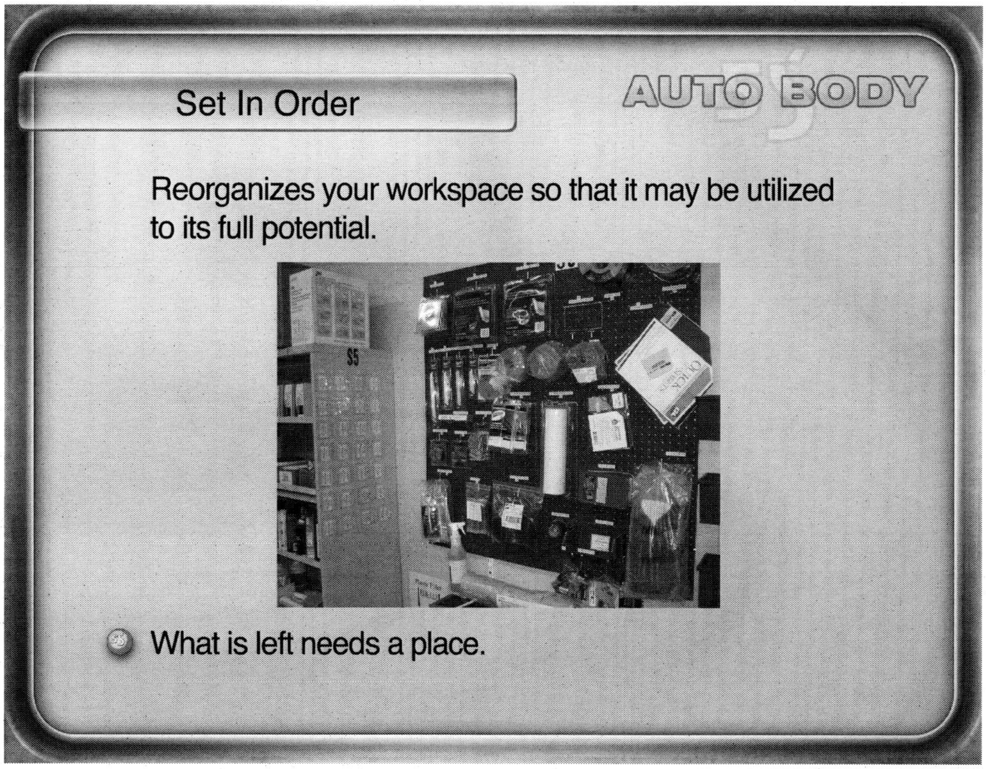

Set In Order

AUTO BODY

Reorganizes your workspace so that it may be utilized to its full potential.

What is left needs a place.

Notes, Slide 20:

_____

_____

_____

_____

Set In Order Action Defined: _____

_____

Additional Example: _____

_____

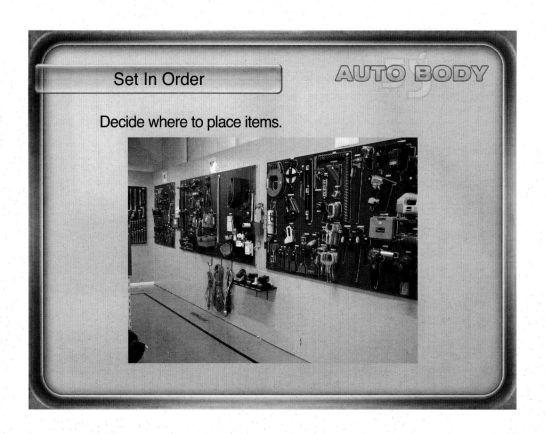

Set In Order

Decide where to place items.

Notes, Slide 21:

_____

_____

_____

_____

_____

_____

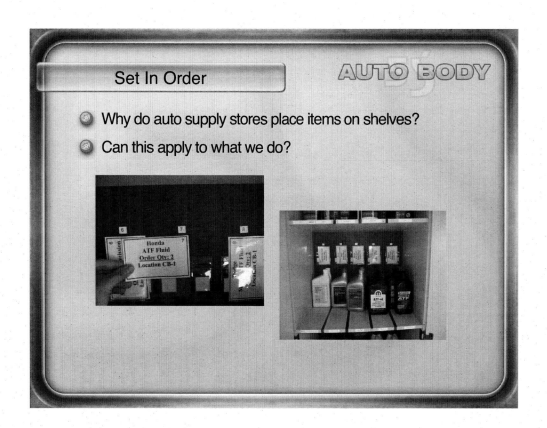

Notes, Slide 22:

_____

_____

_____

_____

_____

_____

Tip:
Try to reach for anything
in your work area. The
goal of Set In Order is
to eliminate reaching.

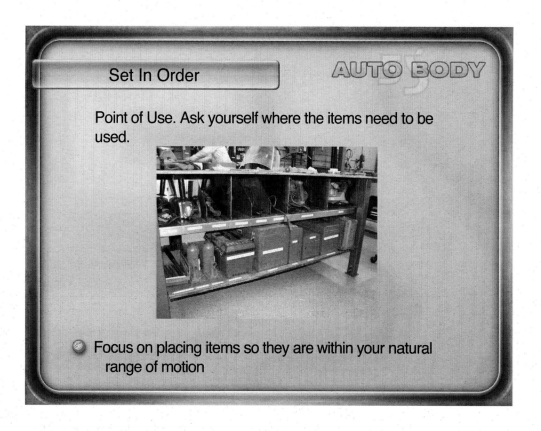

Set In Order

AUTO BODY

Point of Use. Ask yourself where the items need to be used.

◉ Focus on placing items so they are within your natural range of motion

Notes, Slide 23:

_____

_____

_____

_____

_____

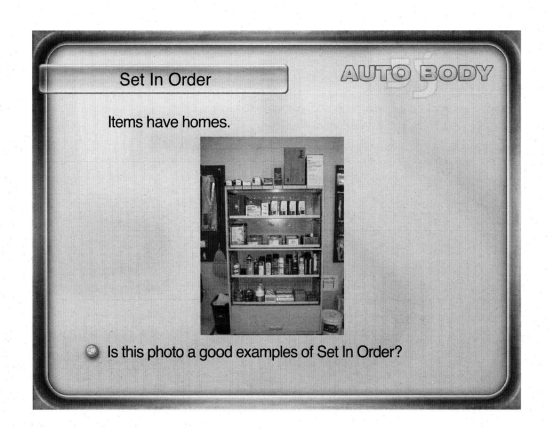

Notes, Slide 24:

_____

_____

_____

_____

_____

_____

Tip:
Use Set In Order to get working, rather than just preparing to work.

Notes, Slide 25:

_____

_____

_____

_____

_____

_____

Additional Example: _____

_____

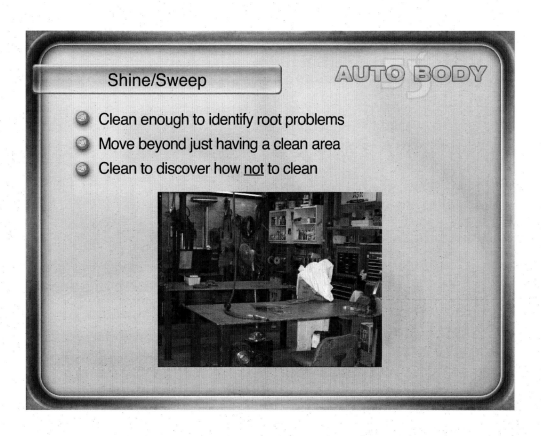

Shine/Sweep

- Clean enough to identify root problems
- Move beyond just having a clean area
- Clean to discover how <u>not</u> to clean

Notes, Slide 26:

_____

_____

_____

_____

Tip:
Remember, we are
cleaning to...

Shine Action Defined: _____

_____

Additional Example: _____

_____

Question:
Why are we cleaning during this workshop?

_____

_____

_____

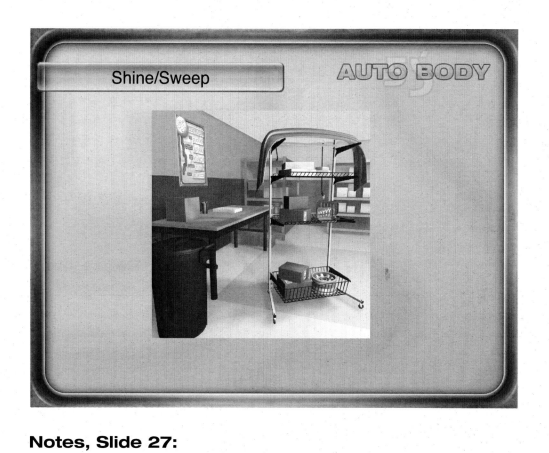

Notes, Slide 27:

Tip:
Combining ideas
together will find solu-
tions to reducing and
even eliminating the
need for shining.

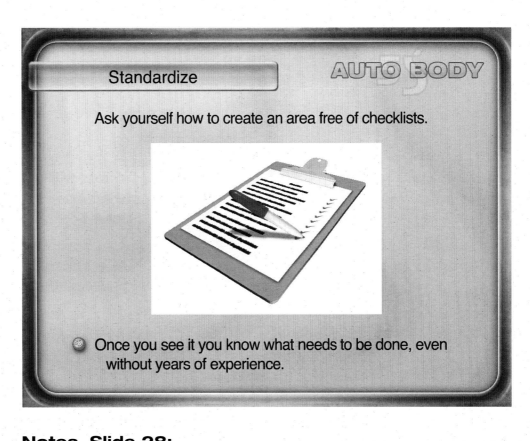

Standardize

Ask yourself how to create an area free of checklists.

Once you see it you know what needs to be done, even without years of experience.

Notes, Slide 28:

_____

_____

_____

_____

_____

_____

Question:

Why are we cleaning during this workshop?

_____

_____

_____

Standardize: Examples

AUTO BODY

Notes, Slide 29:

_____

_____

_____

_____

Standardize Action Defined: _____

_____

Additional Example: _____

_____

Tip:
When creating a standard, incorporate a symbol, color, and/or physical characteristics.

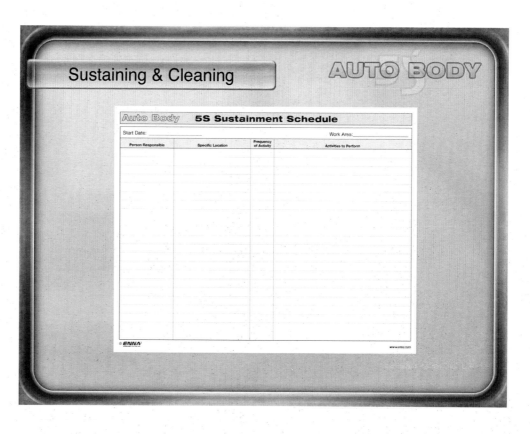

Notes, Slide 30:

_____

_____

_____

_____

_____

_____

Question:

Why is it useful to employ the 5S Sustainment Schedule?

_____

_____

_____

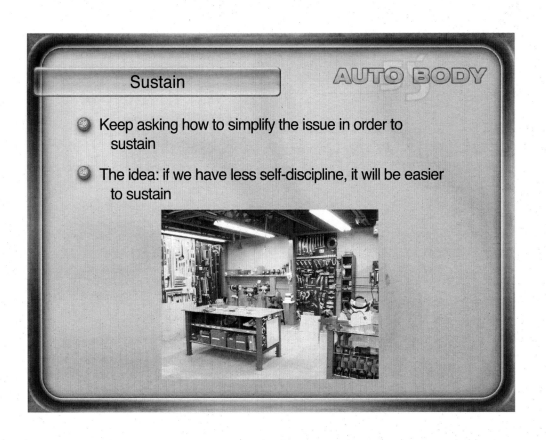

Notes, Slide 31:

_____

_____

_____

_____

_____

Question:

What is the ultimate goal of 5S?

_____

_____

_____

Sustain

AUTO BODY

- Management shows commitment to program
- Everyone leads by being an example of 5S
- 5S is a component to every workshop
- Goal is to have business customers be able to tour your facility
- Use the Evaluating 5S Forms to assess 5S score

Notes, Slide 32:

_____

_____

_____

_____

_____

Sustain Action Defined: _____

_____

Additional Example: _____

_____

Tip:
Use your past employment experience to help develop sustaining changes. Often past examples help develop solutions. Pull examples from the past and see how the team can use them.

Notes, Slide 33:

_____

_____

_____

_____

_____

_____

Long Term 5S Success

AUTO BODY

- Management is expected to be involved
- Involvement of everyone
- 8 Wastes are an integral part of 5S
- Link improvement to financial benefit

Notes, Slide 34:

_____

_____

_____

_____

_____

_____

Question:

5S needs the commitment of who?

_____

_____

_____

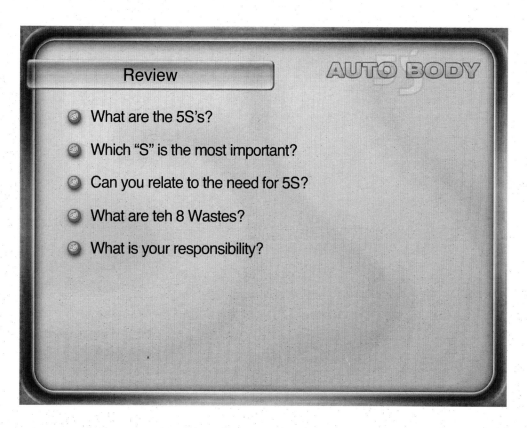

Review

AUTO BODY 5S

- What are the 5S's?
- Which "S" is the most important?
- Can you relate to the need for 5S?
- What are teh 8 Wastes?
- What is your responsibility?

Notes, Slide 35:

_____

_____

_____

_____

Final thoughts on this section: _____

_____

_____

Tip:
Write down the answers to these questions to summarize this section.

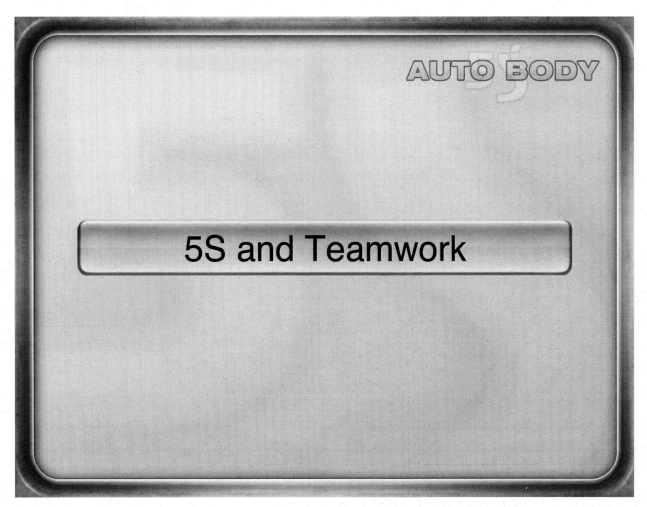

Participant Workbook

In this Section

Now that we have gained some knowledge, we are going to put it into practice.

 **Suggestion**

 Tip

Question

5S Teamwork

AUTO BODY

Steps:

1: 5S Evaluation

2: Sort - Red Tag Activity

3: Set In Order/Straighten - Point of Use Storage

4: Shine/Sweep - Clean Area

5: Standardize - Visual Management

6: Sustain - Refine and Schedule

Notes, Slide 37:

_____

_____

_____

_____

_____

_____

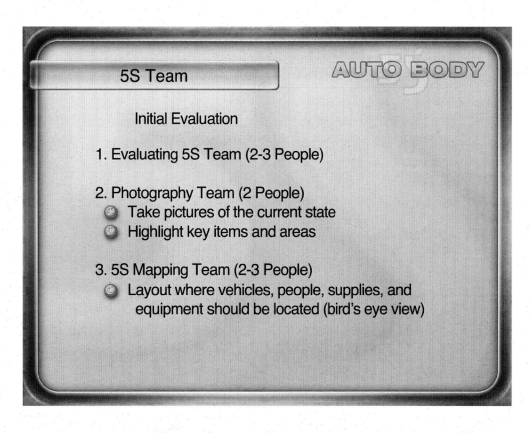

5S Team

AUTO BODY

Initial Evaluation

1. Evaluating 5S Team (2-3 People)

2. Photography Team (2 People)
   - Take pictures of the current state
   - Highlight key items and areas

3. 5S Mapping Team (2-3 People)
   - Layout where vehicles, people, supplies, and equipment should be located (bird's eye view)

Notes, Slide 38:

_____

_____

Team Assigned To: _____

_____

Team Members Names: _____

_____

_____

Assigned Work Area:

_____

Additional Information: _____

_____

_____

Tip:
You will change roles as you move from assessment through to making changes, but your team should stay together.

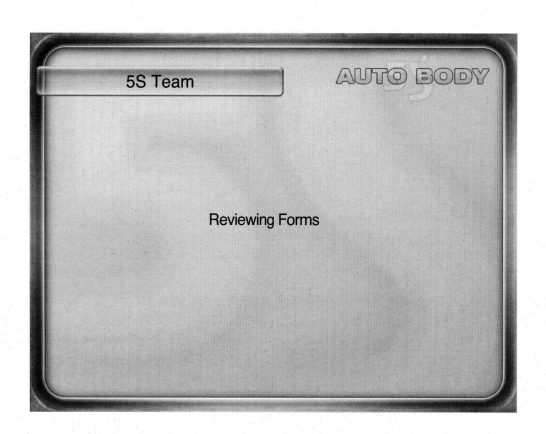

5S Mapping

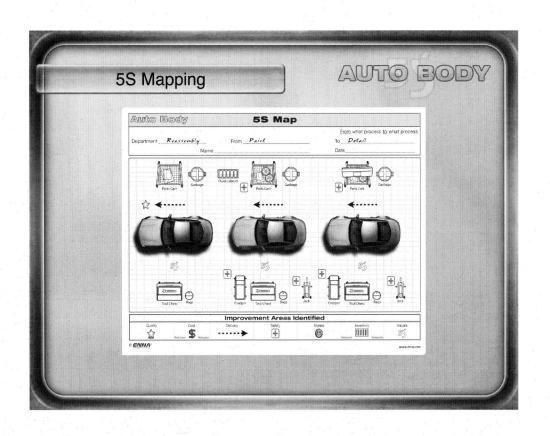

Notes, Slide 40:

_____

_____

_____

_____

_____

Notes, Slide 41:

_____

_____

_____

_____

_____

_____

Tip:
Be critical when evaluating the area; the initial evaluation serves as a baseline for further comparison.

Notes, Slide 42:

_____

_____

_____

_____

_____

_____

Tip:
Lighting is key for photographs. Have the team borrow lights to make the items in the pictures really stand out.

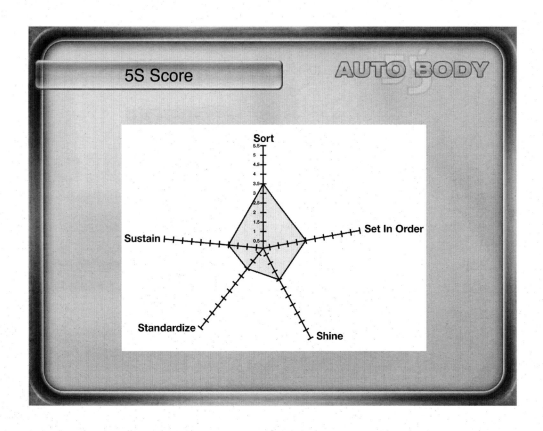

Notes, Slide 43:

_____

_____

_____

_____

_____

_____

Tip:
We should be ready to evaluate our current state.

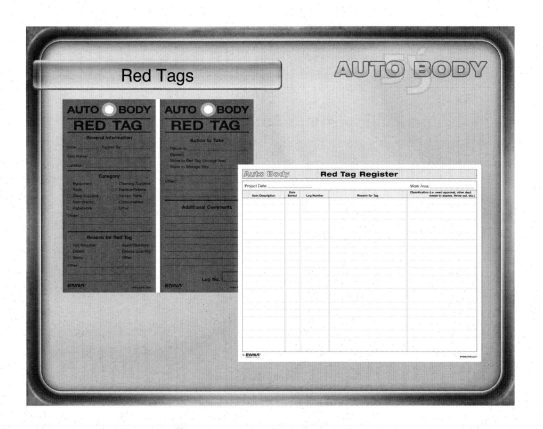

Notes, Slide 44:

_____

_____

_____

_____

_____

_____

30 Day Action Log

Notes, Slide 46:

_____

_____

_____

_____

_____

Tip:

Only place items on the 30 Day 5S Action Log that the team has agreed is an item for that list. Your team should all agree before adding an item to the 30 Day 5S Action Log. You may have to get support from other departments.

5S Sustainment Schedule

Notes, Slide 47:

_____

_____

_____

_____

_____

_____

Tip:
Team members are expected to commit to 5S by providing innovative ways to solve problems.

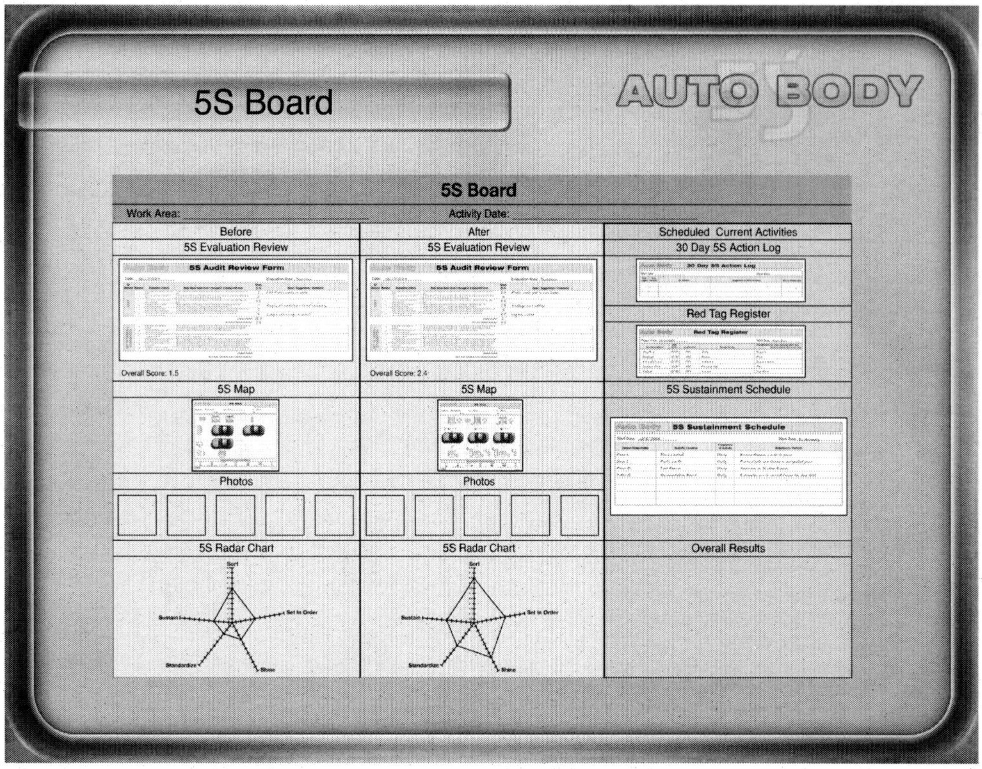

Notes, Slide 46:

_____

_____

_____

_____

_____

5S Assessment

Facilitator: _____   Name: _____

Workshop: _____   Date: _____

Circle or write the answer that best fits the question or completes the statement.

1. _____ 5S originally had _____ S's.
   a) 4
   b) 1
   c) 2

2. _____ What company started what is now known as 5S?
   a) Volvo
   b) Toyota
   c) Ford

3. _____ What is the first S of the 5S's?
   a) Set In Order
   b) Sort
   c) Shine

4. _____ of the 8 Wastes of Lean Auto Body which one is the worst?
   a) Overproduction
   b) Inventory
   c) Motion

5. _____ If a company implements 5S successfully, the need for self discipline is _____.
   a) Eliminated
   b) Reduced
   c) Increased

6. _____ 5S is one of the building block of _____.
   a) Operations
   b) Cleanliness
   c) Lean

7. _____ Why do we clean during 5S?
   a) To inspect
   b) Because it is the right thing to do
   c) To prevent bad parts

8. _____ Inventory exists as _____.
   a) Raw, WIP, FG
   b) GF, WIP, RAW
   c) PIW, WAR, FG

9. _____ The S, Set In Order, allows for a person to have minimal _____.
   a) Work
   b) Waiting
   c) Motion

10. _____ What is the 5S Sustainment Schedule used for?
    a) Recording workshop activity
    b) Recording the cleaning that is needed
    c) Scheduling the next workshop

11. _____ For 5S to be successful we need the involvement of _____.
    a) Top management
    b) Entire department
    c) Everyone

12. _____ The 5S Map provides a simple _____ view of the work area.
    a) Bird's eye
    b) Planning
    c) Outline

13. _____ Extra processing is the hardest waste to find because _____.
    a) There are so many processes
    b) It may initially seem to be a value-added step
    c) It is totally necessary

14. _____ The 30-Day Action Log allows the company to _____.
    a) Document a list of unsolvable problems
    b) List workshop problems to be solved on one document
    c) Demonstrate its commitment to 5S

1:c, 2:b, 3:b, 4:a, 5:b, 6:c, 7:a, 8:a, 9:c, 10:b, 11:c, 12:a, 13:b, 14:b

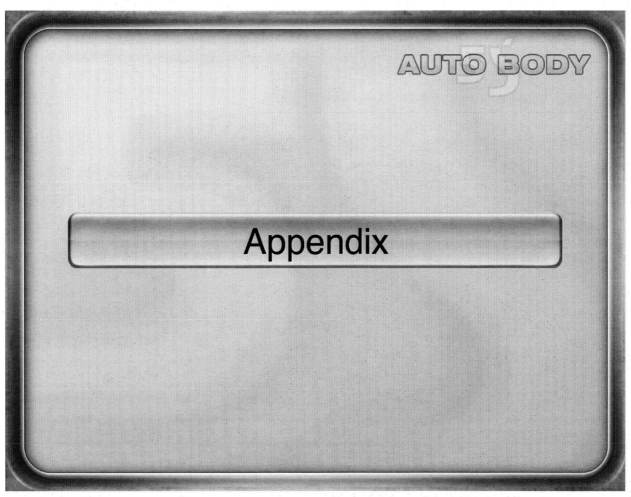

Participant Workbook

In this Section

You will find copies of the forms used in the workshop filled out for your reference.

Before

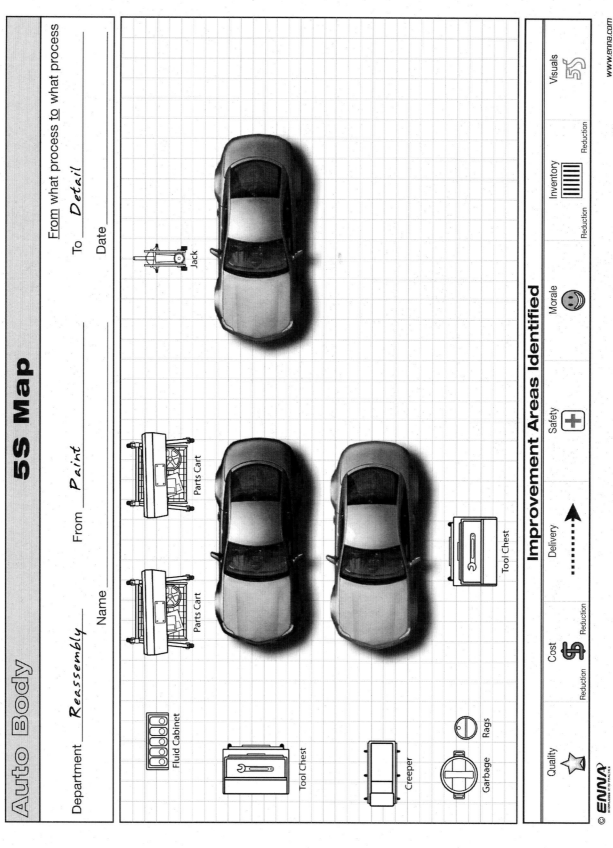

www.enna.com

After

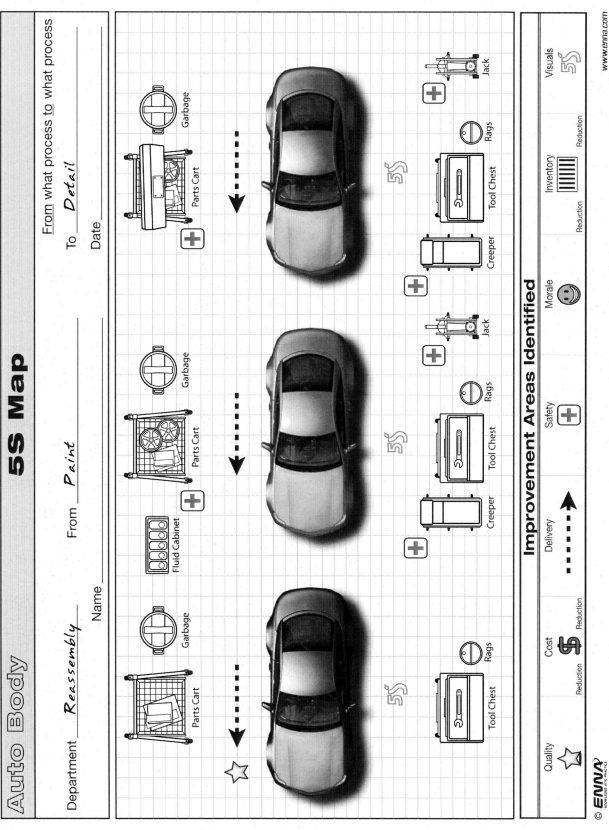

Auto Body

5S Map

Department __Reassembly__   From __Paint__   From what process to what process

Name _____   To __Detail__

Date _____

Garbage   Parts Cart

Fluid Cabinet

Creeper   Tool Chest   Rags   Jack

Improvement Areas Identified

Quality	Cost	Delivery	Safety	Morale	Inventory	Visuals
☆	$ Reduction		✚	☺	Reduction	5S
Reduction					Reduction	

Auto Body 5S Audit Review Form

Date: 12/11/2009

Evaluation Area: Teardown

5S Element	Number	Evaluation Criteria	Rank these items from 1 through 5: 5 being well done	Score (1-5)	Ideas / Suggestions / Comments
SORT	I	Are the aisles and walkways open and clear?	All items that are not necessary or unsafe have been removed from the area where people travel and work.	3	(2) Parts carts in aisle
	II	Is the work area free of any spills of fluids?	Consider whether there are any lubricants, water, oils or other materials that may be hazardous in the work area, on the floor, or under vehicles that are not necessary.	2	
	III	Is the work area free of unnecessary items and tools?	Are items that are not needed been removed from the work zone, i.e. tools, parts, cans, tags, extra items.	3.5	
	IV	Is the work area free of excess consumables/materials?	Evaluate against how many items are in the work area. Assess if the materials, parts, and supplies are currently needed for the repair area, staging area, point area, etc.	1	Empty oil containers in re-assembly
	V	Is the production/ information board active and to what degree?	All jobs in each respective area of the shop are known and displayed. Announcements are current and in presentable shape. Arrangement is straight and placed under appropriate headings.	2	
	VI	Are the area's walls and dividers free of items not used in the shop?	Extra items are not on the walls, dividers, or hanging of signs that are not necessary.	4	Couple extra rags in detail
			Category Subtotal	15.5	
			Sort Score: Subtotal divided by 6	2.5	
SET IN ORDER / STRAIGHTEN	VII	Evaluate any documentation storage.	Only documents to do the job are stored at the work area. Stock is limited and pre-staging is based on known lead-times throughout of the repair shop. Documentation is understandable to outsiders.		
	VIII	How are the shelves, desks, and work surfaces arranged?	All locations of items are labeled, marked, and it is known if they are missing.		
	IX	How are the tools and material used in operations stored?	No items are resting on or under automobiles nor tucked in corners. No items are resting on essential equipment, unknown in cupboards, or other places.		
	X	Evaluate temporary storage containers and staging locations and tidiness.	Parts, re-manufactured, components, and other items are stored in the appropriate place and orientated well for specific stage of the repair process. Items are secure and not causing any danger to the works.		
	XI	Assess orderliness of items on the shop's floor.	Minimal items are sitting directly on the floor and no materials are left around the vehicles. Items that need to be set on the floor are clearly marked and positioned in designated areas clearly outlined.		
	XII	Availability of tools for repair and teardown as well as measuring gauges.	Tools, components, measuring devices, and any fixtures need for teardown and repair are organized in a systematic way to ensure they are easily within reach and if not available are known where they are.		
			Category Subtotal		
			Set in Order / Straighten Score: Subtotal divided by 6		
SHINE / SWEEP	XIII	The storage of gauges and tooling.	Arrangement and storage of all fixtures, tools, and gauges are kept in clean well organized and visual area for storage and no risk of damage or loss can occur.		
	XIV	Clear when equipment needs maintenance and when last maintained.	Machines are clearly marked, highlighted, and labeled. Compliance or check sheets are clean and displayed. Any maintenance is known scheduled; fluid levels, lubrication, and joints are accessible.		
	XV	In each department assess the cleanliness of the work area.	How dust free are the areas. Look under equipment, under vehicles, behind work benches, and tool chests to see if there is garbage and other unnecessary items.		
	XVI	Safety, are areas sectioned off and safe for workers?	Spray shields and physical guards are in active use to keep paint overspray and other sprays within the department. How much paint is getting on the floor. All critical areas are clearly marked to protect workers.		
	XVII	Assess status of equipment in the area. Cleanliness overall appearance.	Are machines, repair equipment, and other vehicles known to be on a maintenance schedule for cleaning and repair?		
			Category Subtotal		
			Shine / Sweep Score: Subtotal divided by 5		
STANDARDIZE	XVIII	Is there visual color diagramming and color coding?	A clear and present color coding system is present in the work areas and across the shop. It's immediately clear that standards are being maintained and improved on.		
	XIX	Assess the access ways in case of emergency.	All emergency systems, fire vehicles, fire extinguishers, and emergency equipment free of obstruction and clear at all times. Access to electrical controls and fuses are known, marked, and free of any obstructions.		
	XX	The aisle ways are bright with light and clearly marked.	Walkways are clearly highlighted for direction, aisle access identified at any moment while in the work area. Transitional areas between the different departments and intersections are clearly marked.		
	XXI	General area has quantity limits for stored parts and are marked clearly.	Heights are marked, quantity of materials are known, and min vs. max is maintained. Shop carts are standardized to hold only parts for one vehicle. Large parts are clearly related to their respective cart.		
	XXII	Is there clear document control of information in the work zone?	All information and documentation is controlled, labeled, and revisions are up to date. There are no label-less binders or work orders in the area.		
			Category Subtotal		
			Standardize Score: Subtotal divided by 5		
SUSTAIN	XXIII	The aisle ways are clean and maintenance is clear.	Aisles are never full of anything and are clear for passage. All vehicle parts are stored in work areas and only in designated storage areas next to aisles therefore allowing accessible movement in the area.		
	XXIV	Illustrations and work area plans are available to compare against.	5S operates a system that allows for controlled change and further improvement of 5S in the work areas. Scoring is kept on each of these 5's and history is present and visible to support future improvement.		
	XXV	Organization is now visible. Tool locations are known and allocated.	No self-discipline is necessary to ensure that all tools, equipment, gauges, and parts are put back in the same spot. No extra effort is needed to sustain 5S in the area.		
	XXVI	Evaluate the involvement of supervisors in 5S.	Supervisors are actively involved in the review process of 5S and are supporting improvement activities of the work areas.		
			Category Subtotal		
			Sustain Score: Subtotal divided by 4		

Total "Category Subtotals" divide by 26 average 5S score: TOTAL

Red Tag Register

Project Date: _12/11/2009_

Work Area: _Parts Room_

Item Description	Date Sorted	Log Number	Reason for Tag	Classification (i.e. need approval, other dept. needs to assess, throw out, etc.)
Shop Rags	12/20	001	Dirty	Supplies
Headlight	12/20	002	Broken	Part
Estimate Forms	12/20	003	Outdated	Documentation
Cordless Drill	12/20	004	Personal Tool	Tool
Cabinet	12/20	005	Unused	Furniture

Auto Body — 30 Day 5S Action Log

Start Date: 2/10/2010

Work Area: Reassembly

Date Logged	Item Number	5S Problem	Suggestion to Solve Problem	Who is Responsible
2/15/10	1	Empty Parts Caddy's are Scattered Throughout the Shop	Create a Designated Location/Mark/Label/ID	Jared F.
2/17/10	2	Technicians Steal Clean Up Tools	Create End of Day Clean Up Tool Boards in Each Area	Henry S.
2/20/10	3	Vendors Cannot Find Their Returned Parts	Visually Designate a Return Parts Area in Parts Room with Vendor Name and Location	Troy G.
2/20/10	4	Towels Used for Soaking Up Water Are a Safety Concern	Fix the Leak Near the Receiving Garage Doors	Jan T.
2/22/10	5	Estimates in Teardown are Not Organized Based on Pick Up Date	Implement Visual Incoming and Outgoing Estimate Staging	Jared F.

www.enna.com

Auto Body 5S Sustainment Schedule

Start Date: __12/5/2009__

Work Area: __Re-Assembly__

Person Responsible	Specific Location	Frequency of Activity	Activities to Perform
Dave L.	Fluid Cabinet	Daily	Ensure Kanban Cards in place
Dave L.	Parts Carts	Daily	Parts Carts are stored in designated place
Peter O.	Tool Boards	Daily	Tools are on Shadow Boards
Peter O.	Documentation Board	Daily	Estimates are in correct folder for 2nd shift

www.enna.com